Christine Owens

Fair Trade: a concept for the equality of all

Table of Contents

General Introduction:

Who made the shoes or t-shirt we wear? Who has produced the coffee we drink and the chocolate in which we eat with pleasure? Before the 1960s, asking yourself this type of question was very marginal. Until English and Dutch non-governmental organizations decided to look into the problem ... And what they discovered was not all rosy: exploited children, poorly paid workers, glaring inequalities ... To fight against these plagues and to create a more harmonious relationship between producers and consumers, these NGOs then decided to think of a way to make trade more just. Fair trade was born ... But it was not until the 2000s that the general public began to discover this concept, on a global scale.

At the international level, fair trade organizations agreed in 2001 on a common definition of fair trade: Fair Trade is a trade partnership based on dialogue, transparency and respect, the aim of which is to achieve a more equitable great equity in world trade. It contributes to sustainable development by providing better trading conditions and guaranteeing the rights of marginalized producers and workers, especially in the South. Fair trade organizations, supported by consumers, are actively engaged in supporting producers, raising awareness and campaigning for changes in the rules and practices of conventional international trade.

To ensure sustainable and universal development, it is necessary to change the rules of world trade. For more than 40 years, organizations working for fair trade have been trying to build their foundations.

Fair trade is therefore an **exchange system with a** clear objective: to ensure fair remuneration for producers in disadvantaged countries so that they can improve their quality of life and develop their business in the long term. In other words, fair trade aims to **reduce inequalities and help the development of poor countries**.

1-What is Fair Trade?

Fair Trade is a movement born in the Netherlands in the early 1960s to promote the balance of trade between North and South. Gradually, this new way of understanding commerce has spread throughout Europe and North America by becoming a global method. The goal today is to help small producers to live off their trade by providing them with decent working conditions and income, to respect the environment and to protect them from the global economy.

Definition

It is therefore difficult to summarize in a few lines all the issues and principles of fair trade as its field of action is vast. Thus, in 2001, the four major international fair trade organizations (FLO, IFAT, NEWS, EFAT) agreed on a common definition:

"Fair Trade is a trade partnership based on dialogue, transparency and respect, the goal of which is to achieve greater equity in world trade. It contributes to sustainable development by providing better trading conditions and guaranteeing the rights of marginalized producers and workers, especially in the South. Fair trade organizations (supported by consumers) are actively engaged in supporting producers, raising awareness and campaigning for changes in the rules

And practices of conventional international trade ".

2-The 10 principles of fair trade

- Creating business opportunities for economically disadvantaged producers
- Applying transparency and credibility in trade
- Developing the individual capacity and autonomy of workers

- Promoting fair trade and raise public awareness
- Commit to a fair price in consultation with the producer
- Practice gender equality in business
- Respect standards of protection of working conditions
- Respect the UN Convention on child labor
- Encourage eco-responsible practices and the protection of the environment
- To maintain "moral" commercial relations.

3-The criteria Of fair trade

3-1 Economic criteria

The fair price must cover both the costs sustainable production and the costs of life, for the producer and his family, and provide a surplus for reinvestment in his business or spared.

At the selling price paid to the producer is added a percentage (either by the umbrella organization in the form of a bonus, either in the form of margin of the producer organization) which will be used for project financing collective development.

In addition to the right price, buyers of fair trade undertake to establish a stable commercial relationship and on the long term, which guarantees a recurrent income to producers, and thus to bring them economic security. A minimum of 5 years based on at least one order per year is fixed. Of course, stakeholders can increase this

Pace.

If producers want it, northern buyers pre-finance orders:

They agree to pay 50% of the amount of the Economic criteria order and 50% on delivery. This prevents producers from getting into debt with banking institutions and to quickly dispose of the fruits of their work.

Transparency and traceability go through dissemination of information from producers (on the modes of production, the conditions work, remuneration ...) and also importers and distributors (on the commercial conditions). The path of products is crystal clear: from production to distribution, the value of the product is known.

- **Work first with the most disadvantaged producers**

This principle corresponds to the desire to allow producers to more marginalized, who are unable to access the market, to sell their production in an alternative circuit.

Artisans du Monde has opted for strong support for small organizations, such as craft organizations on the African continent, at the cost of greater commercial development. Laborious.

3-2 The criteria of autonomy

Producers build their capacity to through training or improvements to their production tool.

The criteria are established in respect of the rights human rights, the right of peoples to self-determination and the non-discrimination of persons.

3-3 Social criteria

- **The right to decent work**

All fair trade actors agree that at least 11 conventions of the International Organization of Labor must be respected.

These agreements concern weekly working hours (48 hours max / week), minimum wages (depending on the wage the country and the cost of living), the minimum age of workers and the fight against child labor (according to the Convention on the Rights of the Child), freedom of expression and freedom of association, the fight against forced labor, working conditions decent and secure.

In addition to these conventions, producers often direct their premium towards the creation of scholarships for their children, access to healthcare, pensions, maternity leave...

3-4 Environmental criteria

Environmental criteria are very important in fair trade practices: reducing impacts environmental issues during the activity; respect for natural resources; the protection of biodiversity; good management of energy, soil, water, waste, transport; packaging management; the prohibition of dangerous substances, GMOs. In some cases, these criteria include a premium for biological conversion.

Thus, the preservation of natural resources is an integral part of the overall development project of the Association of Villagers of N'DEM in Senegal.

All Lao Farmer Products rice production is certified organic, and the company's goal is to promote diversity. Local agricultural products.

3-5 The criteria of awareness

Organizations in the South are sensitizing people at the local level to change practices: by engaging in education, protecting the environment. They are lobbying their political and economic decision-makers for recognition of fair trade and a change in business practices.

- **Campaign, advocate, raise awareness**

Importers and distributors also carry out advocacy actions, especially in partnership with organizations in the South, for changes in the rules political and economic aspects of international trade. They participate in public awareness of fair trade and carry out public opinion campaigns.

The sale of products in fair-trade stores must be accompanied by information to consumers about products, producer organizations, the operation of fair trade channels, guarantees ... But also about the challenge of fair trade by in relation to the issues raised by the dominant international trade ... Information on topical issues for which fair trade actors are committed makes it possible to bring consumers together during campaigns aimed at putting pressure on political and economic decision-makers to change the current rules of international trade.

In addition to the laws of countries that are supposed to protect their inhabitants, and ILO standards, fair trade organizations in the North and South ensure that these criteria are met. The challenge then is to know which guarantee schemes these organizations put in place to ensure this.

4-The labels

To help the consumer to "buy fair", there are now many labels - control authorities independent of brands - which attest that the product is indeed fair trade. They prove that the manufacturer is committed to producing according to quality criteria, respecting the Planet and working conditions.

The problem is that there is currently no official label, which forces us to believe "on word" brand labeled. We must also be wary of brands that create their own label logos, out of control.

Meaning of fair trade

5-North / South Fair Trade

Initially, **fair trade is the** focus of all international business activities, the aim of which is to give producers in "southern countries" what they deserve.

Fair Trade aims to **replace the domination of the North on the South** by real partnerships between these two parts of the globe. Thanks to this type of trade, producers in the "South" would no longer be dominated by importers in the "North".

6-North / North Fair Trade

The **Fair Trade / NE** appeared after the North / South and the same principle as its predecessor. On the other hand, the objective of North / North trade is not to harmonize the relations in favor of the developing countries, but rather for the benefit of the small **local producers**.

In France, this concept of North / North trade has developed a lot as a result of the domination of some large manufacturers over small producers in the food sector.

7-Fair trade products

Today, you can find a lot of **food products** from fair trade:

- Fresh fruits (banana , orange, clementine ...), dried, candied.
- Juice.

- Jams, compotes and fruit purées.
- Delicatessen: oil, rice, sugar, <u>tea</u> , coffee, cocoa, spices, biscuits ...

Fair trade products

Of **fashion items** from this trade are also currently sold men's clothing, women and children, accessories, lingerie...

Cosmetics, wellness, essential oils can also be found as well as **decorative** objects and **furniture** (storage, desks, tables ...).

8-Where to buy these different products?

If in the past it was necessary to visit a shop specializing in **fair trade products**, today you can find them in **organic stores**, on the **internet** and sometimes in **supermarkets**.

As an example, here is a short selection of Fair trade items available on Amazon for those who cannot shop:

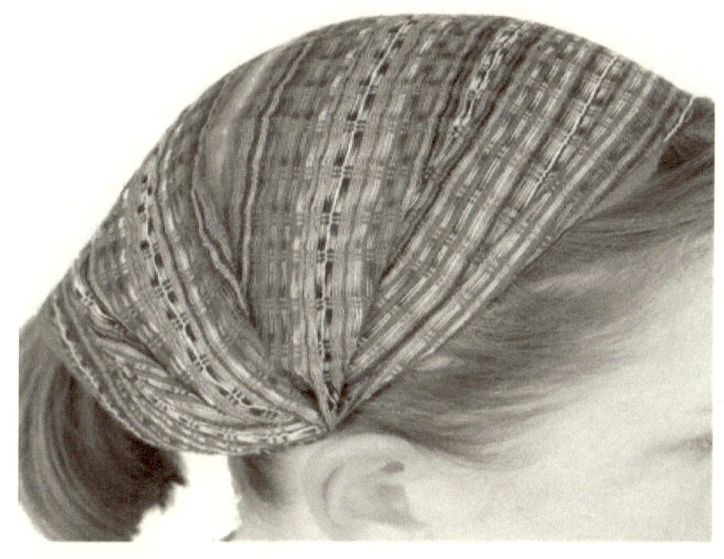

https://www.amazon.com/Cotton-Headband-Scarf-Wholesale-Assorted/dp/B011FJKJ0U/ref=sr_1_17?keywords=fair+trade&qid=1569661648&s=gateway&sr=8-17

https://www.amazon.com/Trade-Telephone-Round-White-Desert/dp/B01LXXP9P6/ref=sr_1_4?keywords=fair+trade&qid=1569661420&s=gateway&sr=8-4

Tota of 20 small hanging birds - Indian decoration - fair trade 85 cm
Suggested retail   https://amzn.to/2ngD3xS price EUR 6,66 https://amzn.to/2ngD3xS

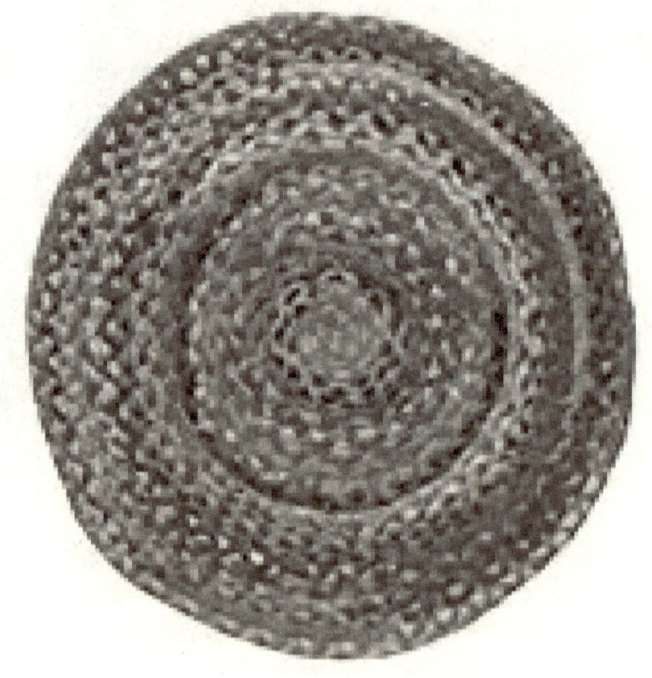

Trade Equi Table Braided Round Recycled Chindi
Cotton Rag Rug, Fabric, Multicolored, 60x60
Suggested   https://amzn.to/2nP71Jw **price**   EUR 20,44
https://amzn.to/2nP71Jw

Winter thick scarf for men and women. They are made of soft wool and luxury. Equitable trade and hand-woven in Ecuador. Extra Long Grand. https://amzn.to/2mp6cH7

Price EUR 29,95   https://amzn.to/2mp6cH7

9-How to recognize them?

At present, there is no own label to identify a fair trade product. On the other hand, certain elements make it possible to differentiate them. Among them, there is the **Max Havelaar label**, the most famous and used label since 1992 fair trade food products as well as fashion items, cosmetics and household items.

Otherwise, other labels like **NGO Oxfam** or **Bio Equitable** also provide a guarantee as to the origin of the products.

10-Business and fair trade

Some members of the **CCTB** (Fair Trade Platform) have been working for several years on the development of a **North / North fair trade** product offering.

Ethiquable and Biocoop, two companies involved, have launched their own North / North fair trade brand.

Business and fair trade

Alter Eco is also one of the pioneers on the market. Let's not Forget Artisans du Monde.

11-Why buy fair?

Buying fair trade products is a win- **win** for both the consumer and the producer. This Trade There fore allows:

- Participate in a **solidarity** purchase and benefit from the guarantee that the producer receives a fair and stable income
- Contribution to the **preservation of the environment**. The products manufactured are made from organic raw materials and in respect of the environment.
- The possibility of knowing the **origin** of the products purchased.
- Participation in a real business relationship.
- Contribution to an equitable **distribution** of wealth.
- Give an example of trade relations based on transparency, respect and dialogue.
- Participation in **improving** the living conditions of disadvantaged producers.
- **Protect** human rights by promoting sound environmental practices and economic security.